Effective Interviewing for Disciplinary, Grievance and Complaints Investigations

How to get what is needed from difficult situations
- An indispensable survival guide

Introduction

The worst has happened - money has gone missing, a complaint has been received, work just isn't getting done - whatever the catalyst you now have to resolve the problem. That means interviewing the staff involved to determine what the cause of the problem was and then proceeding to decide upon the appropriate action.

What you dread, as any organisation does, is being sued. Someone coming along and claiming that they were unlawfully dismissed from their position and that:

> "the investigation was a joke"; "the procedure wasn't followed"; "it was little more than a 'witch hunt'".

This text isn't a guide to the law on employment, which is constantly evolving and would mean that this book would be out of date within a year. No, it's more useful than that! This book will assist you to obtain facts from members of staff and others efficiently, fairly and accurately i.e. this guide aims to tell you what is unquestionably 'best practice' in interviewing. Concisely, objectively and precisely obtaining facts will in turn ensure that whoever has to make a decision about an employee does so having obtained the most specific information thereby making it more likely that they will come to an understandable and justifiable decision that can withstand judicial scrutiny. You don't have to adopt everything within this text but the more you choose to adopt the more robust the interview and investigation will be.

Why am I writing this book? As a result of training numerous organisations within both the public and private sectors; whether small, medium or large in size 'investigatory interviews' have proved to be, in my experience, an area that managers are under prepared and ill-equipped to carry out. Too many individuals believe that interviewing is simply talking to another person but as you progress through this work you will come to recognize that it is much more than just having a conversation.

A word about the layout of this book. What you are holding is meant to be a practical guide therefore it is designed to be dipped into and referred back to whenever you want to. You don't need to memorise the contents instead you need to interact with them. What I hope you will find is that some ideas will be new, some may require a different approach, whilst others may simply be reinforcing your own good practice.

For simplicity's sake I have used the male pronoun "he" but whenever you read this please interpret it to include "she" or "they". It is certainly not because male employees are more likely to be the subjects of your enquiries! Similarly the focus of this book is upon disciplinary interviews but the same principles and techniques I have set out are of equal value in interviews relating to alleged grievances or investigating complaints.

Interviewing is a skill and therefore it can be improved through 3 steps:

- Learning
- Applying
- Evaluating

Before you get underway I would ask from you one attribute as you read through this text: be open to what follows.

All rights reserved. No part of this publication may be reproduced in any material form (including photocopying or storing it in any medium by electronic means and whether or not transiently or incidentally to some other use of this publication) without the written permission of Leslie Cuthbert. Warning: The doing of an unauthorised act in relation to a copyright work may result in both a civil claim for damages and a criminal prosecution.

Copyright Leslie Cuthbert Published by Leslie Cuthbert

www.iiilimited.co.uk

Printed in the UK by Lulu.com

ISBN 978 1 4461 7523 1

Table of Contents

Section 1 - Basic Principles

1.1 Conducting Investigations
1.2 How individuals communicate – The Communication Cycle
1.3 Obstacles to effective communication
1.4 'SEARCH' – Facts v Assumptions
1.5 Key Qualities
1.6 Witness v Subject interviews
1.7 The 'PEACE' approach to interviews
1.8 Fact-Finding v Challenge

Section 2 - Pre-Interview Preparation

2.1 Steps to consider and record
2.2 The BOX model
2.3 A Pro-Forma Plan
2.4 Engage and Explain Ground Rules

Section 3 - The Interview

3.1 Body Language
3.2 Appropriate versus Inappropriate Questions
3.3 Funnelling
3.4 Note-Taking

3.5 Conversation Management Technique
3.6 'Rewinding the video'
3.7 The Challenge Interview
3.8 'Difficult' interviewees

Section 4 - Post-Interview

4.1 Record
4.2 Evaluation of Interview
4.3 Retention of information

Section 5 – Ten Top Tips

SECTION 1 - BASIC PRINCIPLES

1.1   Conducting Investigations

In beginning to think about interviews there are some key points that should be borne in mind when undertaking not just interviews but the entirety of the disciplinary investigation.

"Admissions are not everything"

Let's get one point absolutely clear from the beginning. Getting the subject of a disciplinary investigation to make 'admissions' or a 'confession' of doing whatever he or she is accused of, should never be the sole aim or entirety of your investigation.

To use an analogy I am advising you that admissions or a confession should be the cherry on the top of the cake, not the filling! Ideally your investigation should provide the decision maker, in relation to any disciplinary matter, with sufficient factual evidence to make a determination, regardless of whether the interviewee has confessed to the misconduct, inappropriate behaviour or not.

Why shouldn't simply getting admissions be your aim? Simply because of the power imbalance that exists between you who represents 'the employer' and your employee who is being interviewed. Consider this situation for a moment: in your normal working life your supervisor asks you to do something. You don't want to do it. Would you be confident enough to say that? Would the fear of having a negative comment put in your personnel file or the possibility of your line manager referring to this in your appraisal mean that you would simply agree to carry out their request? For many people that is exactly how they would react and as a result would do as they have been asked. Disciplinary procedures evoke a similar reaction of people wanting to satisfy their employer and as a result they might easily agree to some wrongdoing or mistake because that is what they may perceive their employer wants them to do even though it is not actually true.

Additionally the employee may have the impression, or may have been told by someone, that by admitting the transgression, (even where they haven't actually done anything) is the quickest and easiest resolution and that all they will get is a brief chastisement. They may know someone who in another organisation only received a verbal reprimand for similar misbehaviour and accordingly may not grasp the significance or importance of what is happening.

"Take the blinkers off"

Investigations should always seek to prove two competing hypotheses never just one, what I shall describe as – Hypothesis 1 and negative Hypothesis 1.

For example –

"Hypothesis 1" is that Fred took office supplies home with him without permission;

"Negative Hypothesis 1" is that Fred <u>did not</u> take office supplies home with him without permission.

There are a number of good reasons why you should adopt this approach:

1) It stops you from falling into the trap of being tasked to investigate a matter and assuming that it is, "just another one of those" and subconsciously cutting corners as a result;

2) It helps maintain the investigator's impartiality;

3) It means that you weigh up the evidence fairly rather than closing your mind to elements that 'don't fit' with your theory – as

facts are gathered and examined against each of these hypotheses it is much easier to determine which of the two competing hypotheses appear to make more sense.

"Two heads are better than one"

Two interviewers conducting the interview does not mean an interviewer and a note-taker. As you will see from later on in the book if you want to achieve best practice there need to be two interviewers and both interviewers must perform a proactive role.

One interviewer alone is never going to be sufficient in a disciplinary interview. Of course it is possible for one individual to conduct an interview but if just one person conducts the interview then there is likely to be a deficiency in the questioning and at the same time note-taking/recording of the interview will also suffer. This brings us to the next point….

"Few people can write as fast as someone talks"

If you do not audio record interviews in some fashion the notes you take of an interview will undoubtedly be deficient in that they will not be verbatim i.e. word for word what was said. It is very difficult to write down everything that is said and as a result people tend to summarise what an interviewee has said. As you will come to understand as you work through this book there are distinct dangers in summarising rather than accurately recording the entirety of a disciplinary interview.

In addition if you do seek to write every word you will inevitably have to continually ask the interviewee to pause in order to accurately capture what has been said as most people cannot write as fast as someone can talk. This will give the interviewee the time and opportunity to reconsider what they are about to say and potentially alter it if they wish to. The interviewer should never cut an interviewee off part-way through their answer in order to record what has been said. If they do when they then invite the interviewee to continue what they were saying there is every likelihood that the interviewee, having had the opportunity to consider what they were going to say will respond, "No, that's everything". This is because they will have realised that what they were about to say may be bad for them or make them look foolish or guilty or whatever.

"Memories are fallible"

Very few people have photographic memories or perfect recall. For most of us as soon as an event has happened unless we were specifically seeking to store it in our minds we will struggle to recall everything that took place. Therefore be realistic in your expectations when interviewing people and be very careful of saying phrases like, "But, you must remember".

Just in case you don't believe me and think that your memory is better than the average let's put it to the test.

A bit of fun – Memory Test Part I

Below are two lists. Take 30 seconds to read them and aim to memorise the contents. On page 11 you will be given a third list where you must seek to circle those words in that list which you believe appear in the lists below. Don't go to it now though! Wait at least 30 minutes before turning to the next list and see how you get on. And no cheating!!!

List 1

apple, vegetable, orange, kiwi, citrus, ripe, pear, banana, berry, cherry, basket, juice, salad, bowl, cocktail

List 2

web, insect, bug, fright, fly, arachnid, crawl, tarantula, poison, bite, creepy, animal, ugly, feelers, small

How individuals communicate

Studies have been conducted to determine exactly how people communicate and the results often come as a surprise:

> Over 55% of any communication is NON-VERBAL i.e. it is based upon a person's body language.
>
> Around 38% of communication is based on HOW something is said i.e. the tone of voice, inflections and so on.
>
> Only 7% of communication is determined by the ACTUAL WORDS used.

Although these statistics specifically relate to how people pick up on messages as to whether they are attracted to each other, as opposed to general conversation, the statistics still lead to a number of useful theories so far as investigative interviewing is concerned:

1) Miscommunication and misunderstanding are much more likely to occur in interviews conducted over the telephone as opposed to face to face interviews given the complete absence of non-verbal communication.

2) Individuals are obviously designed to be able to tune into other individual's emotions and underlying points of view regardless of what words someone might choose to use. A good interviewer therefore needs to work to 'tune in' to the interviewee. Research suggests that there are seven basic emotional states, five negative and two positive:

Negative emotional states: Positive emotional states:

- Sadness
- Anger
- Disgust
- Contempt
- Fear

- Surprise
- Happiness

Whilst you are seeking to tune in to the interviewee so too will they, perhaps unconsciously, be tuning in to you. The emotional state they pick up from you may impact upon their willingness to answer questions.

3) How many of us can say that we are 'body language' experts. I have sat in on thousands of interviews and I would certainly not suggest that I am. Yet people still tell me how they could, for example, tell from an interviewee's face that they were lying. Of course when I ask what expression a person's face makes when they are lying the individual seems to have difficulty in describing it! Instead what I will describe in this book are some aspects of your own body language to be aware of and some behaviours by interviewees which may have a degree of relevance to them.

4) It means that the choice of words used although a relatively small factor is vitally important because if you select inappropriate or ambiguous words the likelihood of misunderstanding is greater.

The second biggest element in communicating, as stated above, is the tone of voice and accordingly you ought to ensure that you do not speak in a continuous neutral monotone instead you need to add colour and texture to your questions. In an effort to make you more conscious of this try undertaking the next exercise.

A bit of fun – Don't take that tone with me

Get an audio recording device and then try asking the same question "What happened next?" but with a variety of different underlying motivations as follows:

- A sincere desire to find out what occurred.
- Irritation – as though you've been interrupted from another more important task
- Complete lack of interest in what they might say
- Wishing that someone else was asking the questions instead of you
- Impatience
- Snobbish attitude
- That you need to get away quickly
- That you lack confidence in your abilities
- That you are having an incredibly bad day!

Now listen back to your recording. With each different modulation of question your tone of voice, pitch, inflection, emphasis and emotion should be slightly different. No conscious effort should need to go in to this and equally your message should be capable of being deciphered subconsciously.

1.2 The Communication Cycle

I am amazed at how many people know the phrase "breakdown in communication" but have never considered what this means in practice.

When an individual seeks to communicate with another party there are 4 distinct stages which progress in a circular fashion. They are as follows:

ENCODE   •   SEND

•   •

DECODE   •   RECEIVE

In Western societies the expectation is that the transmitter, the speaker, who has the responsibility to communicate their ideas clearly and unambiguously. Unfortunately some individuals do not understand this or don't have the ability to express themselves clearly and so when you conduct interviews you must take responsibility for ensuring clarity of communication whether you are the speaker or the person listening. It is different in other countries, especially Asian countries, where the responsibility is placed upon the listener to make sense of what is being said.

Every communication starts with the <u>encoding</u> of a message. This involves deciding the language you are going to use e.g. English and the specific words you are going to select to get your message across. Linguist Noam Chomsky referred to language as "a mirror of the mind" and it is important that you therefore focus on the specific words an interviewee uses when they encode their responses to you.

The next stage is the method of delivery – are you going to speak to the person using your voice, are you going to use PowerPoint slides or what? Again studies have shown that people are able to talk at a rate of approximately 150 words per minute considerably faster than someone can write or type. Speaking is obviously the standard means of sending a message in an interview.

The action then shifts to the person being communicated with. Their first task is to receive the message by listening to what is being said; to read the PowerPoint slide; whatever it may be. Interestingly people are able to listen at the rate of 750 – 1000 words per minute which is obviously 5 times as much as anyone is able to talk. With all this 'extra capacity', people therefore have a tendency to decide what they are going to say next, whilst the other person is still talking, rather than focusing their full attention on listening to what the speaker is in fact saying at that precise moment.

> **A bit of fun – Hard listening**
>
> Next time you have a meeting with someone or are listening to a radio programme try to put all your attention in to listening to what is being said. Stop yourself if you start to daydream or your mind wanders at all. Focus only on ensuring that you do not miss nor misunderstand anything that the speaker says.
>
> Afterwards consider how exhausted you feel!

Having received the message it must now be decoded, the meaning must be extracted from it. Everyone comes with their own 'frame of reference' the sum of their knowledge and experiences which will influence how they will interpret what is being conveyed to them.

Once the person who was being communicated with has decoded the message they will then encode their response and the process resumes once more with the roles having been reversed.

Why is it so important that the communication cycle works without interruption or a breakdown in communication?

Simply because when the cycle does falter the interviewer and interviewee may leave the interview with completely different interpretations of what has been stated during the interview. I have lost count of the number of occasions when I have spoken separately to interviewers and interviewees at the end of an interview and they each have a different conception of what has been conveyed during the course of the interview.

Don't believe me? OK, have you ever heard of "Chinese whispers"?

The reason the game "Chinese Whispers" works is because people are so bad at following the communication cycle. Instead of simply repeating the words which they have been told people try to convey the meaning behind phrases but we may all <u>decode</u> and re-<u>encode</u> phrases in a different way depending upon our frame of reference hence why "Chinese Whispers" occurs.

I'm going to set out for you below two very simple, straightforward examples. The first shows how easy it is for the communication cycle to break down and explains why it has broken down. The second seeks to demonstrate how by following the communication cycle you will invariably get more accurate, less ambiguous, information. As you read through this book you will recognise that everything which is set out within this text is designed to enable the Communication Cycle to work as efficiently as possible.

Bad example of the Communication Cycle

Interviewer   –   "Are you happy in your job?"
Interviewee   –   "Well I've been here 10 years."

The Interviewer then moves on to their next issue.

Before going any further take a moment to consider what has been occurred here - why is this a poor example of the Communication Cycle?

There are a number of reasons:

1) The encoding of the question was poor in that it was a closed, leading and ambiguous question (see section 3.2) – what does this word 'happy' mean? [Problem encoding]

2) If we presume the sending and receiving were without mishap then there may well have been a problem in decoding the question given that the encoded answer doesn't actually answer the question that has been asked. You may have drawn an inference from the answer but as you have seen in section 1.4 that is a dangerous step to take. [Problem decoding and encoding]

3) The questioner has moved on when they have not received a clear answer to their question. They have failed to understand/properly decode the response and recognise that they may be drawing an inference from what has been said rather than sticking with the facts. [Problem decoding]

Good example of the Communication Cycle

Question	-	Describe your feelings towards your job?
Answer	-	I'm happy in my role.
Question	-	You say you're happy; what do you mean by 'happy'?
Answer	-	Well I get enough money and enough holiday.
Question	-	How do you feel about the people you work with?
Answer	-	They're OK.
Question	-	What do you mean when you say that they are "OK"?

And so on.

This is a better example of how the Communication Cycle should work. The questioner is <u>encoding</u> his questions using as clear language as he possibly can and is listening to and <u>decoding</u> the responses seeking clarification when the decoding gives an ambiguous or unclear answer.

The Communication Cycle also occurs in a secondary fashion. The interviewer who is taking notes must record down what the interviewee has said which, unless they are taking a verbatim note, means that the Cycle must be gone through again. The act of physically writing down the meaning of what the interviewee has said in response to any particular question will engage the Communication Cycle unless a verbatim record is made. The interviewer must re-encode what the interviewee has said which is often referred to as précising or summarising what has been said. If this is not done correctly it will impact upon the eventual reader's ability to decode the notes and decide for themselves what the interviewee actually said in his interview.

A bit of fun – Memory Test Part II

Don't cheat and turn to page 20 until you have completed this exercise!

Underline the words you recognise below which you believe appeared in the previous lists on page 11:

happy, woman, winter, circus, spider, feather, citrus, ugly, robber, piano, goat, ground, cherry, bitter, insect, fruit, suburb, kiwi, quick, mouse, pile, fish

A bit of fun – Memory Test - Explanation

OK compare what you have marked on the previous page with the lists on page 11.

Chances are that some of the words you thought you remembered aren't in the previous list at all. The words in the original lists simply suggested associated ones which appear in the third list e.g. did you underline fruit and spider?

This is an example of how false memories are created in that they are suggested by related words or phrases.

This false memory effect relates to the power of suggestion and is a danger which interviewers must always be on their guard about. We will return to this later!

Remember*ing* in an interview is therefore a dynamic, narrative process which is influenced by the context and social interaction that occurs between people.

As an interviewer your behaviour and responses may well influence the process of the interviewee's recollection.

For example in a famous psychological study in the 1970s conducted by Elizabeth Loftus (*Eyewitness Testimony*, Harvard University Press: Cambridge 1979) participants were shown a series of slides of a road accident at a junction. Although the slide showing the road junction had a STOP sign present the experimenters sought to subtly deceive participants so asked what the colour of the car was which had driven through the GIVE WAY sign. Later participants were shown two slides of the junction one with a STOP sign and one with a GIVE WAY sign and were asked which they had seen before. The majority said the GIVE WAY sign!

There are obviously a myriad of obstacles to effective communication and it is impossible to list all of the possible ways in which misunderstanding or miscommunication may occur. There are, however, some common hurdles which you should be aware of and seek to avoid if you wish to interview efficiently:

o   Consider the environment. Conducting an interview at someone's workplace may make them feel awkward due to other members of staff knowing what is going on or even worse, listening in on what is being said. This may affect how they encode their responses to your questions or may mean they do not give sufficient attention to receiving or decoding your questions. If you interview them at their home you are not in control of the environment so there may be other people present or the television may be left on both of which will obviously cause a distraction potentially impacting on all 4 elements of the Communication Cycle.

o   Interviewing by telephone as opposed to face-to-face is not best practice but may be the only option. In this instance be aware of the dangers of having even less control of the environment in which the interviewee is talking to you. They may be reading some papers or using their computer whilst talking to you so not committing all their attention to the interview impacting on both receiving and decoding. Alternatively they may not understand or decode something which you have said. Usually if this happens face-to-face you are able to see their body language perhaps they have frowned as a result of lack of understanding. Down a telephone line you may miss this and similarly may miss the opportunity to encode the message in a different way that they might grasp.

o   Interviewing by correspondence (letter or email) as opposed to face-to-face is even worse than conducting an interview by telephone - it actually requires much more information to be clear as to your message and not cause confusion. Think of your own experiences: how often have you received an email that you weren't expecting and been upset or offended by the content? Yet when you speak to the author of the email they explain to you that you have misinterpreted what they meant to convey. This is due to the lack of tone of voice and body language and the ability to obtain instantaneous clarification as to any misunderstanding. For example, what would you interpret from this simple sentence:

> "You are required to attend for a formal interview on Monday at 10.00 am."

On a superficial level you would note that you are being **required**, not invited or requested, to go to a meeting. It is an order, something you must do. You may immediately think that you are in trouble, that it is believed that you have done something 'wrong', that you are going to lose your job or that something serious is going to happen to you. Without tone of voice and body language to put this sentence into context or to add colour to it all sorts of assumptions and imaginings may go through your mind. Yet sentences such as these often populate a standard letter inviting someone to attend for an interview with little thought given as to the reaction it will provoke. As well as these dangers relating to <u>decoding</u> of the letter there are of course the additional external factors of the letter or email not being properly <u>sent</u> or <u>received</u>.

o The first language of the interviewee may not be the first language of the interviewers. Many people believe that the solution to this is straightforward – use an interpreter! In actuality there are numerous other issues which you must consider when undertaking an interview with an interpreter, including the following:

- o Interpreting is for conveying the meaning of one language into another. Translating documents is a different skill and requires a translator. An interpreter should not be used for this function;
- o Be aware that there may be different dialects for a particular language. Geographical variants may need a different or specific type of interpreter;
- o The Communication Cycle is doubled for every question

and answer so there is a greater danger of "Chinese Whispers" occurring;
- Listen to the length of the interpretation. If you have asked a long question and the interpreter has merely said a few words be careful to check that they are interpreting exactly what has been said. Equally the same may be true for the answer if the response from the interviewee is a lengthy one and the interpreter simply says "No" then something is being lost in the translation. Another warning sign of this is when the interpreted answer which you have been given does not answer the question you asked. What I would urge you to do at the start of the interview, when seeking to build a rapport is to set out a series of ground rules including telling the interpreter that they must interpret exactly what you say and that if they are unable to, because a word is unable to be translated, then they must inform you of this and you will re-phrase (RE-ENCODE) your question;
- Even if it is not your normal practice to audio record interviews consider doing so with an interpreter present to prevent any subsequent suggestion that the interpreter did not properly relate the questions or answers;
- If interviewing a person who is deaf and has been since birth they may well have Sign Language as their first language and accordingly having them write down their responses would never be sufficient. Additionally videotaping the interview might be appropriate in a serious enough investigation where sign language interpreters are being used as audio recording will be of little value.

- The interviewee having some form of learning difference (this is the more appropriate term than 'learning disability'). Again this may well impact upon their ability to both encode their message and decode your message. For example, people with dyspraxia (a developmental co-ordination disorder) have difficulty with orientation and new situations. They get easily confused and suffer sensory overload as a result. Alternatively individuals with dyslexia may when reading documents suffer from glare from white paper, have the print fade out as they try to make sense of the document or have double vision when seeking to decipher material. And before you think that you won't possibly deal with people with learning differences the Developmental Adult Neuro-Diversity Association identifies 15% of the population as affected by Specific Learning Differences. The sorts of things you can do to compensate are: ensure the person knows what topics are going to be covered, ask questions in a simple style, encourage them to take their time replying, help them to locate relevant sections of text and don't jump on a hesitance or misunderstanding they may make. If dealing with someone with Asperger Syndrome your interviewing may require even more radical overhaul since they will find responding to open questions even harder to manage. Other changes to make include: not interviewing for more than 20 minutes before taking a break, focusing on what they can do rather than what they can't do and avoid repeating the exact same question simply because you deem the first answer unsatisfactory or incomplete. People may interpret the exact same repeated question as a criticism of their earlier response and may change their response as a consequence, perhaps to an answer they believe is closer to the answer the interviewer wants to hear.

o   Interviewee's inability to read and write competently. It is a dangerous assumption that many employers make that their staff are able to read and write. Giving someone the staff handbook does not mean that they have read it or understood it. When asking someone,

    "Are you aware that there is a policy that governs x?"

    you should not infer from a positive response that they have either been able to read the policy or that they have understood what they have read.

o   People accompanying the interviewee. A challenging aspect in and of itself and something I will return to later. As far as the Communication Cycle is concerned, however, the danger is that they may <u>decode</u> what is said differently and may intervene with their own interpretation of what is being discussed. Alternatively they may interrupt the interview leading to a break in the <u>sending</u>

and <u>receiving</u> of statements.

- o Either party having other events weighing on their minds – for example needing to get away to collect their children from school, having a family member in hospital and so on. This will impact on their <u>encoding</u> of their message, potentially on their <u>receiving</u> it and certainly on their <u>decoding</u> of it. They will likely feel under pressure of time and as a result will not be as thorough as they ought to be.

- o Making the interview inappropriately accusatory or relaxed. If the interview is made extremely accusatory the interviewee may well become guarded in relation to their answers and be very vigilant as to what they are saying. Alternatively if made too laid back the interviewee may not give sufficient thought and consideration to what they are being asked and the answers they are giving meaning that they say the first thing that occurs to them rather than what they truly believe is the accurate response.

1.4 'SEARCH' – Facts v Assumptions

'SEARCH' is the an important acronym designed to help you remember important basic principles for good interviewing.

'SEARCH' stands for:

> Seek Facts not Assumptions
>
> Explore Opinions to determine the Facts which led to them being formed
>
> Accurately record Facts, not your interpretation of them
>
> Refer to Facts not Inferences in your questions
>
> Confirm your understanding of the Facts given
>
> Hold individuals to account on the basis of the Facts obtained

Let's look at each of these concepts in turn in more detail.

Seek Facts not Assumptions

This is first for a reason, because it is the most important issue you should never lose sight of when conducting an interview. Interviews are there to gather facts, they aren't there for you to only confirm assumptions you have already made.

Don't misunderstand me in that I know everyone makes assumptions, after all we couldn't get through life without them, but in conducting an investigatory interview you need to be much more aware of the assumptions that you are making than at any other time in your daily life.

Assumptions come from our backgrounds and you need to be constantly aware of what might influence you to make one assumption as opposed to another.

In an effort to make you more aware of how you as an individual make assumptions go through the exercise on the next page.

A bit of fun – Drawing inferences

Everyone filters their observations of the world through their own self-concepts, biases, prejudices, and knowledge gained from personal experiences (their 'frame of reference').

Read the text that follows and make a note of what conclusions you draw about the Managing Director of the company from the information provided. Then turn to page 22 to compare your conclusions with mine:

You have just arrived at "No Such company" for a job interview. This job sounds ideal. You would be working directly for the Managing Director of the company, who has requested an interview with you. You arrived on time and were met by the Managing Director's secretary, who apologised and said that there would be a delay of at least fifteen minutes as the Managing Director was in a meeting. In the meantime, the secretary has informed you that you are welcome to wait in the Managing Director's private office.

The Managing Director's office is carpeted in blending colours of olive green, brown and orange. You sit in one of two orange club chairs to the left of the doorway. Between the chairs is a low wooden table on which there is an empty green glass ashtray. Next to the ashtray are two matchbooks - one from the Spearmint Rhino club and one from a local restaurant. On the wall behind you is a picture of an old sailing ship in blues and browns.

Across from where you are sitting is a large wooden desk, with a black leather desk chair. A framed advertisement for the company hangs on the wall behind the desk and below that sits a closed briefcase. The black waste basket next to the wall by the desk chair is full of papers.

On the desk are a matching pen and pencil stand and a letter opener. To one side of them is a calculator, and next to that is a brass desk lamp. In front of the lamp is a double metal photograph frame with photographs in it. One is of an attractive woman in her thirties with a young boy about eight years old. The other photograph is a Dalmation dog in a grassy field. In front of the frame is a stack of green file folders. On the desk in front of the chair are a few sheets of paper and a felt-tipped pen. On top is your CV and you notice that the statement of your sex has been circled with a felt-tipped pen.

So what is a fact as opposed to an assumption? A fact can best be thought of as information which has either been recorded in some form of media (a document, tape recording) or is something which has been seen, heard, tasted, touched, smelt, felt or done by an individual.

An assumption or inference in comparison is a statement about the unknown based upon the known. For example you go to enter a fast food restaurant, there is no sign as to whether you should push or pull the door. You **assume** that it is one method - "push" but it is only when you actually perform the action that you discover, as a **fact**, that you need to "pull". It is crucially important to recognise that an assumption may well be correct but it is only proved correct as a result of further investigation, by gathering more information. An assumption is then able to be converted into a fact.

Let us go back a moment to our bad interview example on page 9:

> Interviewer - Are you happy in your job?
>
> Interviewee – Well I've been here 10 years.
>
> The Interviewer then moves on to their next issue.

What has happened in this simple scenario is that the interviewer has made an assumption about what the interviewee has said. They have inferred agreement or acquiescence with what has been said and assumed that accordingly the interviewee is indeed "happy" in their job. Is that a safe assumption for them to have made?

Almost certainly not and it is situations such as this which occur frequently in interviews and which inevitably result in some form of disagreement or dispute in the interview when the topic is returned to –

> Interviewer - "But you said you were happy in your job".
>
> Interviewee – "No I didn't".
>
> Interviewer – "Yes you did".

Don't believe that you would fall prey to such a mistake? Let's see.

I want you to undertake an exercise to make you more aware of how you make assumptions so that you can be more careful in future and stop confusing assumptions with facts.

Read the following paragraph then go to the next page:

> Smith, a psychiatrist with the Trust, was scheduled for a meeting in Khan's office to discuss an incident of aggression at 09:00 hours. On the way to that office Smith slipped on a freshly waxed floor and, as a result, received a badly bruised leg. By the time Khan was notified of the accident, Smith was on the way to hospital for x-rays. Khan called the hospital to enquire, but no one there seemed to know anything about Smith. It is possible that Khan called the wrong hospital.

Having read the paragraph, please classify each of the following individual statements as either a fact or an assumption/inference by ticking the relevant box alongside each statement. The statement can only be a fact or an assumption not both.

		Fact	Assumption
1	Mr Smith is a psychiatrist		
2	Smith was supposed to meet with Khan		
3	Smith was scheduled for a 9 o'clock meeting		
4	The accident occurred on the Trust's premises		
5	Smith was taken to hospital for x-rays		
6	No one at the hospital that Khan called knew anything about Smith		
7	Khan called the wrong hospital		

Was that easy?

Feeling pretty confident?

OK turn on to the next page to see how you did and to understand why the answers are what they are.

Answers

		Fact	Assumption
1	Mr Smith is a psychiatrist		√
2	Smith was supposed to meet with Khan		√
3	Smith was scheduled for a 9 o'clock meeting		√
4	The accident occurred on the Trust's premises		√
5	Smith was taken to hospital for x-rays		√
6	No one at the hospital that Khan called knew anything about Smith		√
7	Khan called the wrong hospital		√

Surprised?

Did you start off the exercise with the assumption that there would be a mix of facts and assumptions? This is exactly the sort of assumption that many people make in relation to a multiple choice test when they believe that not all the answers will be answer "C". In this instance that assumption may well have influenced your decision making.

Let us examine each of the statements in turn so that you can understand why they are all assumptions.

1) Mr Smith is a psychiatrist – if you stated this was a fact it was most likely because you focused on the word psychiatrist and when you read the paragraph you saw the words "Smith, a psychiatrist". What you have not done is to have considered the entirety of the statement though. The statement states that Smith is a Mr, a male. Look again at the paragraph. Nowhere within the paragraph is there an indication of Smith's gender. Yes there is a 50% chance that Smith is male but until you have further information the statement "Mr Smith is a psychiatrist" remains an assumption.

2) **Smith was supposed to meet with Khan** – check the text of the paragraph. Although Smith was having a meeting in Khan's office it does not necessarily mean that it was with Khan. Yes Khan was notified of Smith's accident but it may be that Khan is Smith's line manager. It is not a fact that Khan is whom Smith was supposed to meet.

3) **Smith was scheduled for a 9 o'clock meeting** – although it may be that the meeting was scheduled for 9 o'clock the way the text reads it could also mean that the incident of aggression occurred at 9 o'clock. As it is unclear which is correct the statement must be an assumption.

4) **The accident occurred on the Trust's premises** – this should have been an easy one to spot as there is nothing within the paragraph to indicate where the accident occurred. If you had this one down as a fact you are going to have to be extra vigilant not to fall into the trap of drawing improper inferences.

5) **Smith was taken to hospital for x-rays** – there were 2 assumptions contained within this statement. Did you realise that? Firstly was the assertion that Smith "was taken" when the paragraph does not indicate how he was travelling to the hospital and indeed it might be he/she was doing so alone, under his/her own power. Secondly there is nothing to say that Smith arrived at the hospital.

6) **No one at the hospital that Khan called knew anything about Smith** – here alarm bells should have rung and you should swiftly have ticked the assumption box. Why? Look again at the statement. It is incredibly wide with two parts in particular causing enormous concern – "No one" and "anything". What do these terms mean? They indicate that not a single person in the entire hospital knew the slightest piece of

information about Smith. How could that statement ever be a 'fact' unless Khan spoke in detail to every single person in the hospital?

7) Khan called the wrong hospital – again hopefully this was a straightforward assumption that you spotted. There is nothing in the paragraph to indicate whether it was the correct hospital or not.

Now do you believe how easy it is to make an assumption?

The other real danger with assumptions comes from relying upon them as facts without having got the additional evidence to convert them into facts.

Let me give you an example of what I mean. I am going to give you a number of facts and in relation to one fact I want you to decide what is the reasonable inference that may be drawn from that fact.

Scenario – One day the police are searching in the woods when buried underneath a fallen tree trunk they discover a black plastic bag. Inside that black plastic bag they find a white carrier bag and inside that white carrier bag they find a handgun. They send everything off to their laboratory and get the information back that Mr Robin Banks' four fingerprints from his right hand have been located on the black plastic bag. Taking this fact alone, Mr Banks' four fingerprints having been found on the black plastic bag, what is the reasonable inference that you may draw from this fact?

Turn over to the next page for the answer.

If you said "Mr Banks owned the gun" or "Mr Banks hid the gun" you are way off. You have in fact succumbed to what is known as a 'chain of inferential logic'.

In reality there is only one reasonable assumption that may be drawn from the fact of Mr Banks' four fingerprints being found on the black plastic bag and that is that at some point in his life Mr Banks touched that black plastic bag. That's it. Nothing else.

To get from the fact that Mr Banks' four fingerprints were found on the black plastic bag to the conclusion that Mr Banks had any kind of control over the gun you would have to build inference upon inference. This is an incredibly dangerous step to take in any investigation since as you have seen earlier any assumption may have one or more alternatives.

Let me give you one example of how you could get from this single fact you have, to the inference that Mr Banks was in control of the gun:

FACT - Scientific examination shows Mr Banks four fingerprints on the black bag

INFERENCE – At some point in his life Mr Banks touched the black bag

(This is an inference rather than a fact as it could be that Mr Banks' fingerprints were transferred onto the black bag via some form of contamination)

INFERENCE – When he touched the black bag Mr Banks was actually in control/holding the black bag

35

INFERENCE – When he had control of the black bag the white carrier bag was inside it

INFERENCE – While holding the black bag with the white carrier bag inside it the handgun was inside that.

Therefore it is possible to get to the inference that Mr Banks had control of the gun but every time someone moves from one inference to another there are more and more alternative inferences that could be drawn. This makes relying solely upon Mr Banks' fingerprints on the black bag as evidence that he had anything to do with the gun as a very foolish step and the case as a whole is made weaker the further removed from a fact you go. It is also important to recognise that this is only one possible 'chain of inferential logic' and that there are a myriad of possible explanations or circumstances that might have occurred but our brains seek to find a pattern, to work out some arrangement that makes sense to us despite the lack of facts.

A bit of fun – Drawing Inferences Part II

What conclusions did you reach about the Managing Director?

Here are a few alternative assumptions that people could make given the facts:

1) The Managing Director (MD) is a busy person due to being delayed in a meeting (or the MD may have caused the meeting to overrun due to being late in to work);
2) Being asked to wait in the MD's office is a 'test', part of the interview process to see how you react, what you do (or it may simply be the secretary's temporary solution);
3) The colours of the MD's office are quite an unusual mix – retro/stylish, so the MD is either someone of a certain age or with certain style interests (or it may be that they were chosen by the previous MD or an interior designer and the MD wants to have the colours changed);
4) The MD is a smoker due to the ashtray (or it may be that this is present for people who come in to see the MD);
5) The matchbook from Spearmint Rhino table dancing club indicates a the MD is a man, possibly even someone who objectifies women (or again this may have been left by someone who came in to see the MD);
6) The MD enjoys sailing/boats due to the painting of the sailing boat which the MD would see from their desk (or it may be that again this belonged to the previous MD/is an interior designer's touch);
7) The MD is proud of the company and/or their achievements given the framed advertisement behind the desk (or again it may be that this belonged to someone else, it may be that it is there to intimidate people coming to see the MD);
8) The MD is married with a young son due to the photograph of the woman and 8 year old boy (a classic assumption but a dangerous one in that there are a multitude of possible interpretations – it could be that this is a photograph of the MD herself and her son, it could be the MD's sister and her child or the MD's daughter and child or the MD when he was a boy and his mother and so on);
9) The MD has a Dalmation dog (or again it could be that the dog has recently died or even died some time ago);
10) The MD is sexist in some way given they have circled your gender on your CV (who knows why they circled your gender – this is complete speculation and you cannot know why they circled it without more information).

Explore Opinions to determine the Facts which led to them being formed

How many times have you thought or said the following:

"He was helpful"

"She was uncooperative"

"That was aggressive behaviour"

"He was drunk"

The first point to recognise with all of these statements is that they are all opinions. A decision maker is able to reach a conclusion as to whether or not they are also facts but fundamentally they are a view that has been reached as a result of the recipient assessing another's words and/or behaviour as against their own 'frame of reference'. Remember, in almost all instances decision makers have to come to a decision on the facts; an opinion is just another form of assumption which may or may not be accurate as you have seen above. REMEMBER - Opinions are NOT facts.

When interviewing someone you must seek to keep your own opinions out of the interview as otherwise you lose your impartiality. Instead seek to probe any opinions expressed by an interviewee. In terms of the examples given above the types of follow-up questions which should have been asked are set out below therefore ought to have been asked,

>Answer – "He was helpful"
>
>Question - "What makes you say that?" or "Give me examples of what you experienced that made you form that view"

Accurately record Facts, not your interpretation of them

Just as important as keeping your own opinions out of the questions you ask is the need to record information in your notes accurately and impartially. Unfortunately many people tend to paraphrase in an effort to condense what has been said and in so doing alter the meaning of the text.

For example someone might say,

> "When he came in he slammed the door shut, started pointing his finger at me and shouted at me accusing me of being stupid"

The interviewer might easily record in the notes of the interview,

> "When he came in he was behaving in a really angry way".

Refer to Facts not Inferences in your questions

This is something which I will return to later when you look at Imperfect Syllogistic questions (don't worry I'll explain what it means when I examine different types of question).

For now I want you to recognise the importance of keeping your answers based upon facts and keep inferences and assumptions away from them. Again the advantages of doing this and the disadvantages of failing to focus on this principle is best shown by means of an illustration.

Let us examine the following simple example:

Question - "How long have you been with your Doctor Mrs Jones?"

Answer – "Twenty years"

Inappropriate Question – "So you're happy with your Doctor?"

Stop for a moment and think how you would feel if you were Mrs Jones and you loathed your Doctor. The only reason you stay with him is because your husband has insisted you must as he plays golf with the Doctor. How might you feel about the interviewer's question? Would you feel that the interviewer isn't listening to you? That they have already come to their own conclusions? That you can't perhaps now explain how you feel because the interviewer might not believe you?

These are the drawbacks of asking questions based upon inference rather than fact.

Confirm your understanding of the Facts given

A vitally important element in the interview process and the means by which you ensure that the Communication Cycle is working effectively.

Let us analyse an example to demonstrate this principle in action.

Questioner – "What is your role in the company?"

Interviewee – "I am in charge of Human Resources within the organisation."

Questioner – "You are in charge of Human Resources, what is your job title?

Interviewee – "Director of Human Resources"

Questioner – "What does being the Director of Human Resources entail?"

Interviewee – "Well all disciplinary matters, all recruitment goes through me."

Questioner – "When you say all disciplinary matters go through you what do you mean?"

Interviewee – "I will allocate an investigation manager and a hearing manager to investigate any disciplinary allegation"

Questioner – "OK, so to summarise, you are in charge of Human Resources?"

Interviewee – "Yes"

Questioner – "In terms of disciplinary matters specifically this means that you select an investigation manager and also the hearing manager in relation to that alleged disciplinary offence?"

Interviewee – "Yes and I would also arrange any appeal against a sanction imposed by a hearing manager."

What I hope you note from this is the constant way in which the Questioner returns to the previous answer or answers given by the Interviewee and both checks their understanding of what they have

<u>decoded</u> but also uses that information as a springboard from which to <u>encode</u> their new question. This method is often referred to as 'reflecting' and fulfils both tasks.

Hold individuals to account on the basis of the Facts obtained

This principle comes at the end because in an interview scenario you should not be seeking to challenge an individual as to their account until you have obtained as many facts as possible. You need to drill down into their account, you need to completely 'funnel' their version of events (funneling is described on page 46) in relation to all the various topics you wish to find out about in order to ensure that when you come to put any contradictory facts to them they are unable to assert that you misunderstood them previously or failed to enquire about a certain point.

Again by way of an example let us consider that during your questioning you have obtained from the interviewee, Patrick, the following facts:

> They have worked for the company for 5 years.
>
> They attended an induction programme when they joined the company.
>
> They have attended each of their yearly performance appraisals.
>
> That as far as they are concerned they always arrive on time for work.
>
> That on arrival before doing anything else they would get their 'clocking in' ticket stamped by the machine in the staffroom.

Prior to the interview you had carried out a preliminary investigation and from this had obtained 'clocking in' timecards which showed that instead of 'clocking in' for work at 9 am when the company began work the interviewee's timesheets showed that at least twice a week the interviewee did not have a timesheet stamped before 9.30 am.

In dealing with this potential contradiction of facts the Questioner might therefore handle matters as follows:

Questioner – "Now Patrick you told me that you always arrive for work on time is that right?" [Confirming your understanding of the facts they have given]

Interviewee –	"Correct"
Questioner –	"And that's always the case, is it?"
Interviewee –	"Yes I pride myself on my time-keeping"
Questioner –	"And you also said that on your arrival, before you do anything else you get your timesheet stamped, yes?"
Interviewee –	"Yes"
Questioner –	"Again is that always what you do, every working day?"
Interviewee –	"That's right"
Questioner –	[Handing over clocking-in ticket] "Please tell me what this is?"
Interviewee –	"It's a clocking-in ticket the company uses"
Questioner –	"How long a period does the ticket cover?"
Interviewee –	"It covers a 4 week period"
Questioner –	"Whose clocking-in ticket is it?"
Interviewee –	"Well the name on it is mine so I presume it is mine"
Questioner –	"Why do you say you presume it is yours?"
Interviewee –	"Well because all the clocking-in tickets are kept together and someone could mistakenly have used mine and then continued to use it."
Questioner –	"What were you told about clocking in at your induction?"
Interviewee –	"That you need to be careful to use your own ticket"
Questioner –	"What are the start times shown on the clocking-in ticket you have in your hands?"
Interviewee –	"Generally 08.55"
Questioner –	"You say generally 08.55 are there other start times shown?"
Interviewee –	"Yes there are a few later times"
Questioner –	"Please count up and tell me how many show start times later than 08.55?"
Interviewee –	"There are 9 occasions"

Questioner – "Nine occasions when the start time is shown as later than 08.55. Yet you said a moment ago that you always started by 9.00 am. How can it be that the clocking-in ticket shows 9 later start times?"

And so on.

Having confirmed and validated the answers you were given originally the questioner has moved on to seek the interviewee's assistance in explaining contradictions in relation to the other evidence obtained. The interviewee must either provide an explanation of how this discrepancy has occurred or must change the facts they originally gave and explain why they are altering those facts. Their only other response is to simply state, "I don't know" which is not particularly helpful either to themselves or to the interviewer.

1.5   The Key Qualities of a good investigator and interviewer

Honesty

Accuracy

Impartiality

Why are these the most important qualities for a good investigator and interviewer? Simply because these are the areas in which the interview, the investigation and the interviewer may potentially subsequently be criticised.

An interviewer may be accused of having been dishonest, of having lied in an interview. If they have lied in one situation what is to prevent them from lying in another situation e.g. at a hearing.

An interviewer may be accused of having made a number of mistakes and of being sloppy. If so, how can the decision maker rely upon the interviewee's notes of an interview, of their recollection of events if the interviewer is prone to making errors?

An interviewer may be accused of being biased or of having prejudged a situation. If a decision maker feels that they have shown bias how can their notes be relied upon since they might well have put a different 'spin' on to what was recorded in line with their own preconceptions.

All of these traits are necessary in a good interviewer and investigator to ensure that the facts obtained by them are credible. If ever you are unsure as to what steps to take in a particular situation always ask yourself whether what you intend to do could be described as: honest, accurate and impartial.

There are of course a number of other elements you should keep in mind

when conducting an interview and foremost of these is the need for
flexibility. What I mean by this is the ability to adapt to whatever might
happen in an interview. The adage that you ought to prepare for the
unexpected is an entirely valid proposition so far as interviews are
concerned. I have had a variety of unexpected events occur to me in an
interview:

- an interviewee vomiting;
- an interviewee becoming aggressive;
- the interviewee's accompanying supporter falling asleep;
- an interviewee breaking down in sobs;
- an interviewee sitting in silence and not saying a word to me.

The importance of good planning is something which I will return to
again and again. Only if you are prepared are you able to be flexible and
able to cope with whatever difficult situation might arise.

Remaining calm is another important characteristic. If you get angry as
an interviewer you have lost control of the interview (unless you are
'faking' your anger in an effort to psychologically affect the interviewee)
since you have lost control of yourself. Maintaining control is vitally
important and an element you ought to constantly strive for.

'You get more with the carrot than the stick' is another truism so far as
interviews are concerned. If the interviewee feels that you believe what
they are saying then they are much more likely to co-operate with you, to
continue to answer your questions and be more open. If they feel you
doubt them, that you think them a liar, then they are likely to become
much more defensive, guarded and cautious in relation to what they say.
[Again you ought never to accuse someone of lying in an interview since
you are expressing your view as to the truthfulness of their account when
you have no way of knowing for certain what occurred unless you were
present at an incident – in which case you shouldn't be the interviewer
but rather should be a witness!]

1.6 Witness v Subject interviews

Although for many interviewers their approach will vary between the interview of a witness and that of the subject of the investigation this distinction in methodology is inappropriate.

That is not to say that as an interviewer you should forget that you are dealing with someone who may have more or less at stake as a result of the investigation process but what should not happen is that you allow this to impact upon your honesty, objectivity or accuracy.

Many interviewers choose to interview the subject of an investigation at the final stage in their investigation. Many simply want to give the subject the opportunity to refute or accept what they have discovered from analysing documentation or from the testimony of other witnesses. This can be appropriate but equally it may be valid to have a fact-finding interview with a subject at an early stage in order to identify potential issues early in the investigation. I draw a distinction here between a Fact-Finding and Challenge interview which is explained further in section 1.8.

There are dangers in adopting this approach of conducting a fact finding interview early in an investigation with the subject of it. It may 'tip-off' the subject of an investigation or allow them the time and opportunity to dispose of or alter evidence which could be obtained. Therefore you will need to exercise judgment as to whether or not interviewing in the early stages of the investigation is appropriate.

1.7 The 'PEACE' approach to interviews

P
E
A
C
E

PEACE is a mnemonic to act as a reminder for the following important elements:

· Planning and preparation
· Engage and explain
· Account
· Closure
· Evaluation

The PEACE training method is universally acknowledged as current best practice as it draws on a wide range of experiences – police, lawyers, psychologists, academics, the courts, and civilian investigators. It is not a model which is confined to police interviews alone, however, as some individuals believe. Nor should it be confused with PACE which is the abbreviation for the Police and Criminal Evidence Act 1984 which provides statutory rules for the handling of interviews by the police and other agencies.

At the centre of the PEACE model is a commitment to best practice standards, communication skills, controlling the interview, structure and flexibility. Everything which I have spoken about already.

Let us examine the five distinct stages in the PEACE model in more detail:

Planning and preparation

Cliché time again – "fail to prepare, prepare to fail" – is especially true for interviewing so you ought never to go in to an interview unprepared.

This is a key area that interviewers need to address as interviews which do not obtain all the information sought and flawed investigations generally often have at their root a failure to prepare.

To understand this aspect interviewers must separate planning and preparation in the following way:

Planning is the mental process of getting ready. In planning the interviewer must understand:

· The object of the interview;

· What evidence is already to hand;

· What deficiencies exist and what might be done about them;

· How to prepare a flexible approach;

· What rules must be followed;

· What is known about the interviewee

· What you intend to tell the interviewee about the allegation prior to obtaining their account

In **preparation** interviewers must think about such things as the location of the interview, the environment and the administrative side, such as the collection of evidence, the use of plans and photographs, and whether a second investigator should be present.

Engage

All interviews must start somewhere. As in the planning and preparation, there are two elements – the human side and the administrative side.

The **engage** element deals with the human side, set within the principle that first impressions are very important and set the tone for the interview.

Research demonstrates that there are 2 key factors to encouraging an individual's recollection the first is the use of open questions which I will explain in Chapter 3 but the other is the importance of building a rapport with the interviewee. In my experience far too many interviewers do not spend enough time getting on the same wavelength as interviewees.

Explain

The **explain** element deals with the formalities required by law, rules or regulations, or best practice, and describing to the interviewee how the interview will be conducted.

The engage element is not a soft or weak approach; it concerns common courtesy and using appropriate language and attitudes for the task in hand. Never be insulting or use expletives when interviewing someone. Not only is it disrespectful but it may suggest you are no longer objective.

Account

Having planned, prepared and opened the interview correctly, the interviewer comes to the core of the interview. In the PEACE mnemonic, this is the **account** element – the opportunity to get the interviewee's version of events, their story.

As you will learn in chapter 3.5 an appropriate method for obtaining an individual's account is titled **"Conversation Management"**. This technique offers an opportunity for the interviewers to gather all the relevant facts, clarify what they have been told and accurately summarise what the interviewee has said before going on to challenge any discrepancies or inconsistencies within the account.

Closure

Before the formal closure of an interview, the interviewers should have accurately summarised what has been said, and checked that what has been said by the interviewee has been correctly understood by the interviewers.

The formalities of closure, as required by best practice and common convention must not be ignored. Neither should the opportunity to explain what will happen next, to answer any questions, offer advice or supply information which the interviewee may request.

Evaluation

The post interview evaluation should look at three distinct areas:

- The information obtained during the interview;
- The evidence accumulated during the whole investigation;
- The interviewing officer's reflection on his or her own performance during the interview.

A review of the information obtained during the interview is essential. If it was a victim or witness interview, how does their account fit with other accounts? Are there discrepancies to be investigated? Are there other people to be interviewed? Is more evidence required?

1.8 Fact-Finding and Challenge

Two very different types of interview which again many interviewers do not recognise and continually mix up.

Fact-finding firstly is exactly what the name suggests: finding facts about the matter under investigation. This is the most basic form of interviewing and it is very easy to evaluate whether you have done a good job or not. If presented with a verbatim transcript of a fact-finding interview by simply glancing at the text of the transcript I would be able to determine whether this was in all likelihood a good fact-finding interview or a bad one. If the questions are short whilst the answers are long, this will usually indicate a good fact-finding interview.

Why do short questions and long answers show this? Very simply because in a fact-finding interview the flow of information should be almost entirely one way from interviewee to interviewer. The interviewer is merely acting as a facilitator to the interviewee to guide and prompt their answers. What a fact-finding interview should never be is an opportunity for an interviewer to put certain facts to an interviewee expecting little more than agreement.

The challenge interview is a very different approach. During a fact-finding interview the interviewer may well be presented with facts from an interviewee which do not equate with facts obtained from other sources. For example an interviewee might say that a meeting occurred on 1 May but the minutes of the meeting show that it is said to have occurred on 3 May. The interviewer should not raise such an inconsistency or mistake during the process of obtaining more facts as to do so risks antagonising the interviewee or putting them on their guard. Instead at the end of a fact-finding interview, once all of the topics that the interviewers wished to be covered have been explored, or even better after a short break during which the interviewers may have undertaken follow up enquiries and had the opportunity to prepare specific challenges, the challenges can be put.

This enables all the inconsistencies to be raised at once giving the challenge maximum impact both upon the interviewee and any subsequent decision maker who may be referred to the record of the interview. Although the majority of what follows is designed to assist you with fact-finding interviews I will return to the methods to adopt when conducting Challenge interviews in part 3.7.

SECTION 2 - PRE-INTERVIEW PREPARATION

2.1 Steps to consider and record

Earlier when discussing the PEACE model I set out a number of points that you ought to consider in advance of conducting an interview and I will now go through them in more detail. What I wish to emphasise, however, is the need not just to think about each of these issues but to record your thinking and decisions. This all goes to show that this was a thorough and well-reasoned investigatory process.

Planning:

The object of the interview – you need to be clear as to what the interview is aimed at so that you may communicate this to the interviewee and so that you are able to evaluate whether or not you have achieved the object of the interview.

What evidence is already to hand – this is working out what facts you already have and the source of those facts.

What deficiencies exist and what might be done about them – what assumptions have you made or will you be forced to make and what evidence might you obtain in order to change these assumptions into facts. This is vitally important because this interview may well be the only means to obtain these particular facts.

How to prepare a flexible approach – this is considering what you will do if. Every time you conduct an interview there is the opportunity to learn for the next interview

What rules must be followed – you need to be certain as to what your organisation's policies and procedures say and that you follow this explicitly. (Alternatively if you depart from these rules you must explain why it is that you had no option but to do so.)

What is known about the interviewee – how long have they been with the organisation, have they been interviewed before, what is their personality like?

What you intend to tell the interviewee about the allegation prior to obtaining their account – there are no rules as to what you must or must not reveal to an interviewee prior to the interview. As a general rule you ought to avoid telling the interviewee everything you have learnt from the investigation to date since this may well influence the answers the interviewee gives. Equally, however, you must tell the interviewee something about the allegation as they need to have some idea of what the interview is going to be about.

2.2　The BOX model

This is a straightforward means to structure a fact-finding interview to ensure that all the information which you seek has been obtained.

The analogy I would draw is that of a newspaper which has a series of headlines to draw the reader's attention to the various stories. This is the principle that the Box Model relies upon. By means of a sequence of one or two word "Boxes" you break the interview up into a series of more manageable sections each of which are capable of being 'funnelled' (outlined in section 3.3).

As an example, if I was asked to find out what took place in someone's life on a certain day – say 30th June - I could break that topic up into a series of smaller topics. One method would be as follows:

| WORK |

| HOME |

| PLAY |

Another method could be:

| MORNING |

| AFTERNOON |

| EVENING |

There is no right or wrong way to prepare a Box Model approach. What is important though is to seek to make each Box a topic which is capable of being probed and is not simply answered by one question or, alternatively, is too big a topic to fit within just one box. Like Goldilocks said in relation to her porridge you want a topic size that is "just right". In addition you need to ensure that you are happy with the order of the Boxes but again there is no right or wrong way to order them you merely need to choose an order that is logical.

A bit of fun – Put your Boxes in order

Let us assume you are to interview someone and find out as much information as possible about their favourite movie.

What sequence of boxes would you create?

Again there is no minimum or maximum number of boxes or order of event that you must select. Once you have made your Box Model turn over to see an example I would suggest.

A bit of fun – Put your Boxes in order Part II

Interview topic – "Their Favourite Movie"

PLOT

Not simply genre since this could be answered by just one question.

PEOPLE

Covering characters, actors, director, people they saw the movie with.

LOCATION

The setting both place and time but also where it was filmed.

PRODUCTION

Covering awards, release date and so on.

FAVOURITE

The reasons why it is their favourite movie.

2.3 A Pro-Forma Plan

What follows is a simple template which you can use to prepare for interviews. Not all of the terms within the template have been explained yet so I would urge you to finish reading the remainder of the book before returning to this section.

Lead Interviewer:	Secondary Interviewer:
Date of Interview:	Focused Open Question to begin interview:
Purpose of Interview: Fact-Finding/Challenge Witness/Subject	
Nature of allegation/complaint:	Interviewee's details:
Facts Already Established from Investigation to date:	Facts to be Established:

Information <u>received from</u> Interviewee prior to interview in relation to allegation/complaint:	Information <u>given to</u> Interviewee prior to interview in relation to allegation/complaint:

Interview Plan – Box Model   Key Questions per 'Box'

…………..………………
…………..………………
…………..………………

…………..………………
…………..………………
…………..………………

2.4 'Engage and Explain' Ground Rules

The following is a checklist of points which you should ensure you cover with an interviewee before moving to the Account phase.

i) Check everyone present has switched their mobile telephones off so you are not going to be interrupted.

ii) Explain how the interview is to be recorded i.e. by written notes, tape recorder or whatever.

iii) Confirm what will happen to the record after the interview.

iv) Ask everyone to introduce themselves.

v) The interviewers should indicate their roles.

vi) If the interviewee is entitled to and is accompanied by a friend/colleague with them ensure you make clear what that person's role is during the interview.

vii) Check with the interviewee if they have any external factors that may influence their concentration during the interview e.g. are they under any time pressure perhaps because of the need to collect children from school, are they feeling well (if they have been unwell recently), if the interview room is small or cramped would they like a window open or to sit near a door. Make sure that they are aware that they may request a short break during the interview if they need one.

viii) Confirm what the purpose of the interview is.

ix) Confirm what the allegation is that is being investigated.

x) Confirm what was told to the interviewee in advance of the interview, if anything.

xi) Explain the structure of the interview i.e. a series of topics and that both interviewers will be asking questions and that at the conclusion of each topic there will be a summary of what has been said before moving on to the next issue.

SECTION 3 - THE INTERVIEW

3.1 Body Language

Lots of people believe that they are able to read another's body language. I would always urge you not to judge other people against anything you may have read or been told in terms of 'body language'.

For example – you might have been told that if someone crosses their arms whilst talking to you this is a sign that they are being defensive. Well yes, it can be but equally it may simply be because they find it comfortable to have their arms crossed. Alternative meanings exist for all of these 'signs' also:

- a lack of eye contact ("gaze aversion")
- fidgeting
- sweating
- nervousness
- aggression
- face reddening
- stammering
- twitching

There are certain aspects of how you hold yourself though that you need to be mindful of:

♣ Lean forward and make eye-contact with the interviewee to show that you are interested and listening to what they are saying (although not to the extent that you are staring at them without breaking their gaze!).

♣ Nod your head at various times to both encourage the interviewee to keep talking and again to demonstrate that you are listening and taking in what they are saying.

♣ Do not fiddle with pens, papers or anything else which might distract the interviewee.

3.2 Appropriate versus Inappropriate Questions

Appropriate Questions for Fact Finding Interviews

Wide Open Questions – these might also be thought of as Examination questions. They are the types of questions with wide parameters which invite and allow the interviewee to speak at length on the topic. Examples are questions which begin: "Describe", "Tell me about", "Explain", "Compare" and so on.

E.g.   Tell me about the events of 25th May from when you awoke until you went to sleep that night?

Open Questions – a more focused form of question which nevertheless does not suggest the answer to the interviewee. The simplest way of remembering these type of questions is by the acronym '5WH' which refers to:

Who?

What?

Where?

When?

Why?

How?

E.g.   Who was at the meeting?

What was discussed at the meeting?

Where did the meeting take place?

When did the meeting end?

Why did you attend the meeting?

How were the minutes of the meeting circulated?

Closed Questions – are questions which require and request a simple "yes" or "no" response. Did you, do you, could you, would you, can you, will you and so on. Closed questions have a purpose and that is to clarify matters but they are also used unintentionally and inappropriately on occasion.

E.g. "Was anyone else at the meeting?"

is an appropriate use of a closed question in that you are seeking to clarify whether anyone else was at the meeting.

An inappropriate use of a closed question is as follows:

E.g. "Could you tell me what happened at the meeting?"

This is inappropriate as in an effort to be polite the interviewer has altered the question from a wide open question into a closed question. If the interviewee is listening and responding accurately to what is being asked their response should be "Yes" or "No". How would you feel if an interviewee responded in that fashion to you?

I presume that you would be annoyed, irritated at their response and perhaps even suspicious at what you see as either evasiveness or trickery. Yet the interviewee would have done nothing other than to have answered the question. What people rely upon are interviewees volunteering information, offering explanations and data which is unasked for. That doesn't always happen hence the need for this book!

Instead your simple solution is to replace phrases like "Could you" or "Would you" with PLEASE. The question then remains both polite and Wide Open:

E.g. "Please tell me what happened at the meeting?"

Another point to make here and another cliché to make it with – 'silence is golden'. Always remember this concept because once you have asked a question give the interviewee the time to respond to it. Many interviewers may ask an entirely appropriate open question only to immediately follow it up with alternative answers as they are uncomfortable with a pervading silence. This takes the responsibility to give an answer away from the interviewee and instead presents them with the easier task of selecting the response they wish to give. For example –

Questioner – "How long did the meeting last?"

Interviewee thinks.

Questioner – "Was it 10 minutes, 30 minutes, an hour, longer?"

Interviewee – "30 minutes"

Remember you want short questions and long answers in a fact finding interview. If the reverse holds true – long questions and short answers it may appear as though the interviewer is lecturing the interviewee and may lead to the interviewee being even less communicative. Focus on obtaining from the interviewee what they know about the subject not on the telling the interviewee what you already know!

Inappropriate Questions for Fact Finding Interviews

Ambiguous Questions – as mentioned earlier these may appear to be very simple closed questions but in fact they often hide a lot of ambiguity within them for example:

"Are you *friends* with Joe?"

"Was that the *best* course of action?"

"Do you feel that was *reasonable*?"

Each of these questions are unclear because of the vocabulary used in that everyone has their our own view as to what being a "friend" means e.g. does it mean someone you simply say hello to? Does it mean a person who you go out for drinks with? Someone whose home you visit? Someone who is a 'friend' on your Facebook profile?

Leading Questions – the difficulty with these questions is that they suggest the answers within the question itself. They are invariably also closed questions to which the interviewee might simply respond yes or no. Leading questions give information to interviewees which could be useful to them should they wish to be untruthful and also may give the interviewee the perception that the interviewer is biased.

For example – "Were you the person responsible for putting the money in the safe?"

Multiple Questions – a common problem that occurs when an interviewer asks questions without having thought through the question in advance. Interviewers will start to ask a question and then as they realise it is not as focused as it ought to be they add additional parts to the question.

For example – "What is your job, your role, your main responsibility?"

Rhetorical Questions – these are in fact 'non-questions' to which there is clearly only one answer, and whose function is in actuality to express the views of the questioner rather than to obtain any actual information.

For example – "You're not seriously expecting me to believe that, are you?"

Hypothetical Questions – the biggest problem with this question is that whatever answer is given will likewise be hypothetical when what any interviewer is seeking is facts.

For example – "If I left £500.00 on this table and left the room and you could take the money and no-one would ever know that you were the person who took it, would you take it?"

This will lead to the interviewee giving not only a hypothetical answer but the answer they believe you want i.e. "I wouldn't take the money" thereby demonstrating their honesty.

Similarly rather than asking someone,

> "What would you do if you felt under pressure?"

to gain a factual response it would be better phrased to ask,

> "What have you done in the past when you have felt under pressure?"

Imperfect Syllogistic Questions – my personal pet hate and one I often look out for when evaluating interviewers. This is where the interviewer is allowing their assumptions and inferences to direct the questioning rather than keeping their questions focused on facts.

Firstly let me explain what a syllogism is. A syllogism is a conclusion based on deductive logic. When you are presented with two or more statements you are then able to form a conclusion from combining these two or more statements.

For example -

Proposition 1 – Socrates is a man

Proposition 2 – All men are mortal

Deductive conclusion – Socrates is mortal.

An imperfect syllogistic question is therefore a question based upon an assumption rather than on a fact.

For example -

Appropriate Wide Open Question - "How long have you been with your Doctor Mrs Jones?"

Answer – "Twenty years"

Imperfect Syllogistic Question – "So you're happy with your Doctor?"

From the factual answer given by Mrs Jones (that she has been with her Doctor for 20 years) the interviewer has drawn an assumption (if she has been with him that long she must be happy with him) and has then gone on to ask a question based on that assumption rather than the fact.

> **A bit of fun – Spotting Stupid Syllogisms**
>
> Next time you are listening to an interview taking place perhaps a television interview or someone is asking you questions focus on picking up any imperfect syllogisms that people may make.
>
> You can often spot them because the interviewee may respond to the question with "No, you've misunderstood me...."

Inaccurate Questions – this goes back to the principle I examined earlier of accurately recording the facts stated by an interviewee rather than paraphrasing or summarising incorrectly what you have been told either by the interviewee or a previous interviewee.

3.3   <u>Funnelling</u>

This is an incredibly simple but effective means of finding out information about any particular topic which you may know nothing about in advance of asking questions. This is a method of providing a structure for your questioning without working out in advance every single question you would need to ask the interviewee. There are 3 distinct stages as set out in the diagram below:

Wide Open Question(s)

Open (Probing) Questions

Closed Questions

The most straightforward way of explaining how this process works is by means of an example. Let us take the concept of interviewing 'James' about a meeting he attended where a decision to purchase "New Company" was made. You will already have gone through the initial "engage and explain" phase as described earlier (pg 33) and you are now examining this single topic. [For illustrative purposes, James will not be a difficult or challenging interviewee but rather just someone who will answer questions appropriately without necessarily volunteering information. Additionally I will indicate the type of question that has been asked.]

Questioner (Q) and Interviewee (I)

Q - OK James, I now want to ask you about the meeting which was held in relation to "New Company". Please tell me everything that you can remember about this meeting. {Wide Open Question}

I - Well we met on 2nd April 2008 to discuss the purchase of "New Company" and after some heated discussion the vote was in favour of buying "New Company".

Q - You said "we", who was present at the meeting? {Open Question}

I - Apart from myself Steven, Maria, Lee and Andrea.

Q - What are their surnames? {Open Question}

I - Steven Fielding, Maria Horsfeld, Lee Fry and Andrea Aster.

Q - Apart from Steven, Maria, Lee, Andrea and yourself was there anyone else present? {Closed Question}

Q - Where did the meeting taking place? {Open Question}

I - At the head office.

Q - Why was the meeting taking place at the head office? {Open Question}

I - As that was where Maria was working that week and so we had to have the meeting there.

Q - You said that the meeting was on 2nd April 2008 but when did the meeting start? {Open Question}

I - 10.00 am

Q - How long did the meeting last? {Open Question}

I - 2 hours

Q - 2 hours exactly or was it longer or shorter? {Closed Question}

I - Well I know I was out of there by 12 pm as I was meeting someone for lunch at 12 pm and I wasn't late.

And so on…..

The advantages of funnelling –

- o The interviewer knows precisely where the interview is going and where it has been.
- o The interviewer is better able to maintain control.
- o The interviewee is able to see progress taking place.

3.4 Note-Taking

How you should record notes of an interview and what you should capture in those notes is often a thorny problem for many interviewers.

Firstly in terms of structuring the record of your interview if you adopt the Box Model and funnelling approaches the order of your notes is made much simpler because just as with a newspaper you will have a series of headings under which you will be able to record what the interviewee states. So if one box had the heading "Role" similarly when writing the notes you would have a heading of Role underneath which you would record the responses given to the questions asked about this topic.

What you ought to write down is equally straightforward to state but is more challenging to achieve simply due to the physical constraints of actually writing. The following list contains the minimum information that ought to be found within your notes (compare what is listed here to what you may normally put in your notes):

Date of the interview

Commencement time of the interview

Conclusion time of the interview

Location of the interview

Persons present

Role of persons present

Confirmation that the record is being made at the time

The purpose of the interview (which should be stated during Engage and Explain phase)

The allegation being investigated (again this should be stated during Engage and Explain)

Clear detail as to what, if any, documents are shown to the interviewee

All questions and answers (do not join the two together)

Any non-verbal responses (nods or shaking of the head)

What will happen after the interview

The offer of allowing the interviewee to read and sign the notes at the conclusion of the interview

If that offer is taken up, their signature confirming that they have read and agreed with their notes or alternatively their statement as to what they disagree with in the notes

Anything said or done before or after the actual interview which has not been recorded elsewhere, for example, their asking after the interview if they are going to lose their job.

3.5 Conversation Management

This is the methodology which allows the interviewers working as a team to maintain control of an interview even when faced with a difficult interviewee.

The Process

Lead interviewer asks first focused wide open question and obtains the interviewee's agenda. (The interviewee's agenda is a recognition that everyone has certain topics or issues which they will wish to discuss in an interview. This is why sometimes interviewers may get frustrated because they wish to talk about one subject but the interviewee wishes to discuss something else.)

Lead interviewer opens first topic on interviewee's agenda with open question. i.e. you deal with the topics the interviewee wants to talk about first.

Lead interviewer rigorously probes (5 WH questions).

Second interviewer rigorously probes (5WH questions).

Second and lead interviewer provide an accurate summary of what interviewee has said.

Lead interviewer moves on to second topic – **above process repeated for each topic on interviewee's agenda.**

Lead interviewer moves on to interviewer's agenda – **above process repeated.**

If inconsistencies or discrepancies in interviewee's account, move to 'challenge' phase.

Stage one: First account

It is important to obtain a full account of the interviewee's involvement, including the circumstances before and after, which may be of evidential value.

The interviewer should begin by asking a **focused open question**, framing the topic or events they want the interviewee to talk about. The interviewer then listens to the reply without interruption. As previously mentioned the first question must be pre-planned to ensure that it starts and finishes where the interviewer wants. The purpose behind this 'free recall' is to establish a number of factors at the beginning, which will then allow the interview to progress in a logical and controlled fashion.

The following advantages may be obtained using this approach:

> being allowed to talk freely can relax a tense interviewee;
>
> people become accustomed to talking and giving information;
>
> an interviewer gets the 'whole picture' at the beginning;
>
> it allows the interviewer to check the story with other information already at hand;
>
> it helps to focus on subsequent relevant information.

A good open question to start off with can result in an overview of the circumstances being investigated.

If the reply finishes short of the response required, prompt the interviewee to continue.

If the reply is too brief, then make one more attempt to get more detail by rephrasing the question and requesting more detail. e.g. *"There is obviously a lot more you can tell me so I want you to start at the beginning and tell me what you did in more detail."*

Stage two: Review

The purpose of the review stage is to assess information and decide if the plan of interview is still relevant, and to split the interviewee's account into **boxes** in a chronological order.

The interviewer may identify some **boxes** that fall outside the anticipated sequence of events. These will also require **rigorous probing**. They may include:

o   Topics
o   People
o   Events

Stage three: Account

The purpose of the account stage is to get the interviewee to give a more detailed account of each of the **boxes** in turn in their own words. The interviewer should start with a specific open question within the a **box** which they have identified as being 'safe' i.e. non-threatening to encourage the interviewee to talk freely.

Example:

"Tell me everything you know about this bloke"

Reluctant interviewees may have to be prompted with a few open questions, not probing questions, at this point. Probing questions **at this point** are not recommended as they put some interviewees on the defensive from the outset.

Probe

During this part of the structure, the interviewer utilises 5WH open questions and carefully chosen closed questions in order to extract as much relevant information as possible. It is extremely important that the interviewer maintains a disciplined path throughout this part, keeping to the topic selected. New information may arise which is relevant to the enquiry but this must be set aside for the moment, stored and developed in another box.

It is also recommended that the interviewee is not challenged at this stage. If the interviewer does not believe the information being related, or has other information which contradicts what is being said, challenging the interviewee should be delayed until the challenge phase of the structure.

Alternatively, if the interviewee is giving information which corroborates what is known, or which can easily be checked, then the rigidity of probing in that area may be relaxed and another topic approached.

This is a systematic examination of their account, including any mitigating circumstances.

The interviewer should now examine what they have been told in more detail to assess the accuracy and reliability of the information, either by the presence or absence of mistakes, contradictions or impossible "facts", or by comparison with other evidence. This detailed questioning of the account is referred to as **rigorous probing**.

Stage four: Examples of probing

For best practice the interviewer should follow these guidelines:

o   Explore the account one stage at a time **(box after box)**
o   Do not move on until the current box has been rigorously probed
o   Ask a majority (80%) of open questions
o   Avoid leading questions
o   The interviewer should avoid trying to persuade the interviewee to agree with them
o   The interviewer should avoid answering their own questions

- o Avoid disclosing information that may influence any answers
- o Avoid challenging any apparent lies or mistakes as they arise
- o Clear up ambiguities
- o Concentrate and show that they are listening
- o Ask questions in a logical, chronological order
- o Avoid arguments
- o The interviewer should not be distracted from the information they require – be persistent and firm, but not aggressive
- o Ask the interviewee to pause and return to the topic if they are digressing into irrelevant areas
- o Make notes of what is said so that the interviewer does not get confused

Important

If the interviewee has not mentioned a topic that the interviewer wants to cover, the interviewer should **not** introduce that topic until they have finished probing all the areas that the interviewee has mentioned. There may be a very good reason why the interviewee has not raised that topic: they may not know anything about it; they may think the interviewer is not aware of it and they would prefer to avoid it; or they may be lying and that topic may not fit in with their story and the interviewer may cause the interviewee to alter the rest of their account before having had a chance to probe the unaltered version. However, the interviewer must not forget to cover these areas before completing the interview.

Stage five: Summary

This phase is used to summarise what has been said during the account phase. Summarising the relevant points raised through probing allows the interviewer to:

- o check their own comprehension and picture of the interviewee's account
- o assist interviewees to understand precisely what they have communicated
- o gather their thoughts before proceeding to the next box
- o instigate further information from the interviewee

- o show interviewees that they are being listened to
- o give an opportunity for interviewees to check, alter or add information
- o record and structure their interview records in a logical sequence
- o minimise the opportunity to change their account at a later date
- o to confirm the interviewee's account one point at a time
- o to confirm the interviewee's own words

Investigating officers should start their investigation with an assumption that witnesses are open and honest. However, if the interviewer has evidence which contradicts the account given, the interviewer should not rush into a premature challenge as it can be tactically more advantageous to identify **all** the discrepancies **before** the challenge phase of the interview structure. This is not pre-judging the interviewee or presuming that the interviewee is lying but rather is ensuring that no issues are left unexplored prior to proceeding to the challenge section of the interview.

The use of this method allows the interviewer to establish the truthfulness of the information being received. It also provides a safety element for the interviewer; ensuring witnesses are given the opportunity to change their story if they have been untruthful initially.

When the interviewer is completely satisfied that a **box** has been fully and rigorously probed, it is important to summarise all the evidentially important points the interviewee has told them. This has the effect of closing down the interviewee's room to manoeuvre in the challenge stage of the interview.

When summarising try to use the interviewee's own words as this will be more "familiar" and less threatening to them and it will not alert them to any discrepancies in their account.

To provide the most potent challenges later in the interview, the interviewer must ensure the summary is confirmed one point at a time and not in a cumulative fashion.

On completion of the summary move on to the next **box**. This is referred to as a "link".

Once the account has been exhausted and the interviewer is satisfied it is appropriate to move on to another topic, the information should be logically linked to the next section the interviewer wishes to develop.

3.6 'Rewinding the film'

People normally focus on what they perceive to be the most outstanding features of any incident, but they may not provide sufficient detail for the interviewer who is looking for unique information that will help build up the complete picture.

The object of 'rewinding the film' or 'rewinding the video' is to gain more detail and check the accuracy of an interviewee's account. Each time a witness is asked to give an account there is the potential that new information will be discovered but at the same time the individual may get bored at going over the information again and again.

By changing the order of recall, the interviewer encourages the interviewee to rely on their actual memories rather than rehearsed ones and to examine events from a different perspective. In trying to recall what happened in reverse order, the interviewee has to concentrate on the pictures in their minds to find their way back to the beginning.

The interviewer must ask the interviewee to give an account of what happened in reverse order, from the last part of the incident back to the beginning.

The benefits of rewinding the video are:

a) It is a further recall attempt using a different route to avoid irritation or boredom.
b) It requires more concentration and therefore makes the witness work harder.
c) In trying to link one part of the incident to its preceding part, the witness will need to focus on smaller details.
d) It avoids scripts i.e. a prepared version of events which the interviewee has memorised either deliberately or sub-consciously.

In some cases a witness may not understand exactly what the interviewer requires in this situation the interviewer can use one of the following descriptions to kick start the rewinding the video process:

"Think of what happened as a video recording and imagine that you are watching it in reverse order..."

or

"It's like retracing your movements when you have lost something and you are trying to remember when you last had it..."

Witnesses may come to a premature halt whilst giving their account which may be due to the unusual nature of this task. Should this occur the interviewer is able to prompt them with ***"and what happened before that?"***

Once again the interviewer should not interrupt.

3.7 The Challenge Interview

I have already set out earlier what the Challenge Interview is but here I will set out how to go about conducting a Challenge Interview.

Think about the timing of the challenge. As stated earlier an interviewer should not normally challenge an interviewee whilst they are giving their account. Doing so might discourage them from continuing to give their explanation. Whether to challenge at the end of a particular topic or wait until the interviewee has provided their full account will depend on the circumstances at the time but ideally after the first fact finding interview phase the interviewers ought to take a break. The interviewers then need to plan the challenges ensuring that they will point out each inconsistency, lie or discrepancy one at a time.

Each challenge should be presented in order, either chronologically or in order of impact and after challenge the interviewee should be given the opportunity to offer any explanation they wish to make and to produce any supporting evidence if they have it.

What is crucial, however, is to avoid argument and the best way of achieving this is by adopting a problem solving approach. Present the challenge as a problem which you require the interviewee to assist in solving. The interviewer can explain that there are aspects of the interviewee's account that they wish to explore further in light of other information already obtained. That way, the interviewee is not put on the defensive and is better able, if they so wish, to change their account, or add to it, without embarrassment and without losing face. The interviewer may then go on to ask for an explanation of any discrepancies. The interviewer should not try to give an explanation of why the discrepancies have occurred especially not by accusing the individual of lying. If they are lying and it is 'obvious' that they are lying then that will be the view the decision maker will reach. The interviewer does not need to express that opinion themselves.

All challenges should be given in a neutral tone, in a clear, short way.

3.8 'Difficult' interviewees

There are numerous ways in which interviewees may prove difficult to control.

There are also several events that may happen which can prove challenging to cope with if you haven't considered and prepared for them:

An interviewee wishing to talk about something 'off the record' with you;

An interviewee wishing to get into a debate as to the legal definition of certain terms;

The interviewee indicating their desire to audio-record the interview;

The interviewee seeking to question and challenge the interviewer;

The interviewee arguing as to the nature or scope of the investigation;

<u>Certain points to remember when handling difficult interviewees:</u>

You are never required to accept the first answer someone gives. You are always at liberty to probe and return more than once to a point. You must be careful, however, that persistence does not become bullying or worse insulting or gratuitously demeaning questioning.

People often believe that they can 'tell' when an interviewee is lying. It is very difficult to do so and making judgments as to body language or facial expressions is not straightforward. Research suggests that people take longer when they are lying than telling the truth but not so much longer that you are going to be able to notice i.e. 1.8 seconds as opposed to 1.2 seconds. Do you believe that you would be able to identify a 0.6 second difference?

In addition research suggests that eye contact and hand movements are easy to control so liars use these signals to convey the impression they want.

The best advice I would give in relation to handling difficult interviewees is by means of a popular culture reference. Think about Columbo, the police officer brilliantly played by Peter Falk. Before you start to laugh let me explain. By feigning incompetence Columbo managed to subvert the inherent dominant position of being the police officer investigating a crime. Therefore never be afraid to ask 'dumb' questions or to state ignorance during a fact finding interview. You can demonstrate just how much you have been listening and how you have been assessing what has been said when you reach the challenge phase of the interview process.

Two particular personality types you may come across are:

Introverted also described as: Avoidant or Dependant. They are often perceived as quiet, withdrawn or reserved.

They will often be very uncomfortable during the interview appearing stressed and anxious. Generally they are respectful towards authority figures and make bad liars as they are too anxious. If dealing with someone you determine may be introverted bear these points in mind:

- Take even more time to establish a rapport with them and to create an atmosphere of trust;

- Avoid domineering them. In some cultures if you are in a position of power and that culture respects authority they may find it very difficult to disagree with your statements or conclusions;

- Don't be afraid to make physical contact i.e. a touch on the arm to comfort them;

- Don't judge them.

- Focus on possible internal pressures how they feel about matters as if they are feeling guilty this may lead to a need to confess.

Extraverted also described as: Antisocial, Narcissistic or Histrionic. They are often perceived as confident, arrogant or self-centred. Often they will be good liars (or feel at ease lying), will be manipulative and although they may show anxiety they will rarely feel 'guilty' for anything they have done. In addition if someone is narcissistic they may be boastful or arrogant with a superficial charm and will expect or demand special treatment. If dealing with someone you determine may be extraverted bear these points in mind:

- ♦ You must be well prepared and confident because they may be keen to challenge your accuracy of points;

- ♦ Be a good audience as they may want to show off;

- ♦ Put emphasis on the quality of the evidence you have when conducting the challenge phase;

- ♦ Help them to find their own benefit to answering your questions.

Remember if you are dealing with someone who has done something wrong they will often seek to do adopt one of three defence mechanisms to their inappropriate behaviour:

- Minimisation – aiming to reduce their responsibility for what happened
- Projection – pushing part of the blame onto another
- Rationalisation – essentially that the 'end' justified the 'means'.

A good indicator of whether the person you are interviewing is being truthful or deceitful is to consider what information the individual is giving you. A <u>truthful</u> person will typically provide you with **any** information they may know about the incident. <u>Deceptive</u> people on the other hand seek to <u>limit</u> the information they provide to you.

Listen to the words they use people who are telling the truth tend to use the word "I" a lot more and give a lot more specific. People who are seeking to lie will distance themselves and ramble more in generalities.

For example,

> "I didn't do it" - may be truthful
>
> "How can you accuse me of that?" – may be lying

In comparison with controlling your hands or eye contact controlling the words you use and they way you say them can be much harder.

Therefore interviews where you ask many more wide open and open questions generally result in more verbal cues to someone's deceit. This is partly because you are not giving information to the interviewee by your questions. Also it is because interviewees find such interviews more challenging cognitively in that they have a higher cognitive load or, put simply, they have more to think about! It is far easier for difficult interviewees to simply say yes or no to a closed question so don't give them the opportunity.

SECTION 4 - POST-INTERVIEW

4.1   <u>Record</u>

As indicated earlier (section 3.3) I would urge you at the conclusion of the interview to ask the interviewee to sign the notes of the interview before leaving the interview. There are 2 profound advantages to adopting this course of action.

Firstly it forces you when making notes to write not just for your own benefit but for the potential reader both the interviewee and any potential decision maker. This encourages both accuracy and impartiality of what you record.

Secondly by offering the notes while matters are fresh in the interviewee's mind it is more likely that they will agree with the contents there and then. Many interviewers do not ask interviewees to sign the notes at the end of their interview and instead will go away and type up the notes and send them to the interviewee some days later. This invariably gives the interviewee the opportunity to reflect upon what they have said and when they sometimes see what they said 'in black and white' with the benefit of hindsight they may often decide to dispute the record either disbelieving that they could have said something or realising that they shouldn't have said something and now wish to renege on what they said.

For those people whose notes would be unintelligible to anyone else you need to improve your handwriting. Your notes are never simply your notes. It is crucial that they are comprehensible to others especially if you are not audio recording the interview since they represent the original evidence of what was said. If you are the only person that can decipher them then you put yourself or your organisation at risk of someone asserting that words contained within the text are not in fact the words which you suggest they are.

4.2 Evaluation of interview

I) The interview – what did you get

II) The investigation as a whole – what else do you need to do?

The following are some useful questions to guide your evaluation of the interview and of the investigation as a whole:

o   How did our planning and preparation work?

o   Were our objectives achieved?

o   What new information has been obtained?

o   What do you need to crosscheck with the information you have already obtained?

o   Is there likely to be a need to re-interview that individual?

o   Is there now sufficient evidence to make a decision on the investigation?

o   If not, what further investigation is required?

o   Has that individual suggested other lines of enquiry e.g. new witnesses, who may need to be interviewed?

o   What explanations were put forward for any contradictions/discrepancies?

III) Finally evaluate your own performance as an interviewer – ask your colleague who conducted the interview with you how you did?

4.3 Retention of information

Retaining the interview record

Your organisation is likely to have a policy or procedure which gives guidance in terms of how long you should keep copies of an interview record. You need to know what the guidance says and to follow it but if your organisation does not have such a policy, I would suggest that you keep the notes and paperwork relating to such an interview until any possibility of judicial proceedings being brought by the disciplined party has expired.

If you are unaware of how long this period is then seek advice from your Human Resources or Legal departments or external advisers but I urge you to retain everything relating to the investigation in one place.

SECTION 5 – TEN TOP TIPS

On the next page is an aide-memoire list that summarises many of the lessons in this book and is a sheet you can use as a reminder before every interview you conduct. I put it as the last page as I know many people often flick to the back of a book to see how the story ends!

Think of it as a checklist and use it to help evaluate your performance at the conclusion of any interview you conduct or are involved with

In ending it would be traditional to wish you luck with your future interviewing but as you have now seen luck is irrelevant! If you follow the guidelines set down in this book you will succeed in conducting exemplary disciplinary interviews which will mean that they are far more robust and able to withstand judicial scrutiny if the employers decision to sanction the employee is subsequently challenged.

TEN TOP TIPS

1. Be prepared
2. Be flexible
3. Be honest
4. Be professional and presentable
5. Understand the Interviewee's point of view
6. Let the Interviewee tell their story
7. Listen to the Interviewee's account giving them the attention they deserve
8. Speak their 'language'
9. Say <u>everything</u> with respect
10. Keep control

Printed in Great Britain
by Amazon.co.uk, Ltd.,
Marston Gate.